Quilting Guide

A Beginner's Guide to the Basics of Quilting so that You Can Start Creating and Designing Your Perfect Patterns (History of Quilting, Terminology, Needed Supplies and More...)

By Nora Amlani

© **Copyright 2019 - All rights reserved.**

The content contained within this book may not be reproduced, duplicated or transmitted without direct written permission from the author or the publisher.

Under no circumstances will any blame or legal responsibility be held against the publisher or author for any damages, reparation, or monetary loss due to the information contained within this book. Either directly or indirectly.

Legal Notice:

This book is copyright protected. This book is only for personal use. You cannot amend, distribute, sell, use, quote or paraphrase any part, or the content within this book, without the consent of the author or publisher.

Disclaimer Notice:

Please note the information contained within this document is for educational and entertainment purposes only. All effort has been executed to present accurate, up to date and reliable, complete information. No warranties of any kind are declared or implied. Readers acknowledge that the author is not engaging in the rendering of legal, financial, medical or professional advice. The content within this book has been derived from various sources. Please consult a licensed professional before attempting any techniques outlined in this book.

By reading this document, the reader agrees that under no

circumstances is the author responsible for any losses, direct or indirect, which are incurred as a result of the use of information contained within this document, including, but not limited to, —errors, omissions, or inaccuracies.

Contents

Introduction 1

Chapter 1: The History of Quilting 4

    Hawaii 4

    The United Kingdom 6

    Australian Quilting 10

    Japanese Quilting 11

    The French Tradition 12

    South African Quilts 15

    The United States of America and Canada 16

Chapter 2: The Technical Bits 20

Chapter 3: Quilt Decorating 37

Chapter 4: Distinct and Crucial Quilts Throughout The World 41

Chapter 5: Quilts, Births, Marriages and Deaths 44

Conclusion 48

Thank you for buying this book and I hope that you will find it useful. If you will want to share your thoughts on this book, you can do so by leaving a review on the Amazon page, it helps me out a lot.

Introduction

Quilting is as old as the hills, and for many, it has that terrific mix of domestic requirement, social cohesion, and craftwork and commemoration.

Quilting techniques do not differ tremendously throughout the world, however, the designs are mainly particular to a nation, or a society, although the conventional American patchwork designs have actually ended up being liked worldwide.

It is terrific to have such a craft, which is a way of handing down traditions among womenfolk generally, and which has an end product that can both look stunning, and keep you warm during the night.

An exception to this is, obviously, the Hawaiian quilting tradition, which started under the tutelage of the missionaries, and developed into a way of recording the Hawaiian beliefs and lives. Their quilts talk of their gods, their departed spirits, the new members of their society yet to be born, and the primary historic and cultural occasions of their society. Their use of the wonderful flowers and the love of their culture provide Hawaiian quilting with a really wonderful and valuable quality.

In chillier environments, the quilting circle was an opportunity for the ladies to come together, to discuss the significant matters of the day and to offer vital assistance for each other. The brand-new inhabitants in The United States of America were hardy and tough. The majority of them needed to start from scratch. Homes needed to be constructed, and furnished, and nowadays, almost everything needs to be grown or made.

Needlework was an extremely crucial ability for a lady. Without this, they would not have the ability to make their clothes, and would not have the ability to make the soft furnishings that not just 'make a house into a home' but are needed for keeping out draughts from doors and windows, and for keeping everybody warm during the night.

When societies ended up being more established and there were cash and time available, the quilting circle would make quilts to celebrate particular occasions, and together produce truly big quilts that would decorate the walls of the buildings that functioned as community centers.

And obviously, the social network was important. The older women would hand down their abilities as needlewomen, and designers of quilts and other crafts. More notably, they would hand down important knowledge about family life.

Childbirth, medicines for typical health problems, cooking and how to grow herbs and veggies-- this was the sub-text, and the extremely crucial function of the quilting circle.

Clearly, at various times, and various locations, the women would have different subjects that would prevail over the quilting circles' conversations. The quilting circle was prevalent. It was essential, it was valuable and social, and it produced terrific pieces of work for people and for communities.

Nowadays, lots of women reside in relative social seclusion. Maybe more so within the much more heavily populated metropolitan environments where the majority of us live.

Perhaps we ought to rekindle the spark-- and begin brand-new quilting circles-- everywhere !!

Chapter 1: The History of Quilting

Hawaii

Hawaiian quilting is said to have actually begun when the wives of 2 chiefs were presented to quilting by missionaries on board a boat. Hawaiians would not naturally have actually started to quilt for domestic usage, as quilts were not required in the warm Hawaiian environment.

The missionaries showed the Hawaiians how to cut up fabrics into pieces, and after that, stitch them back together. This the Hawaiians found rather thriftless, as they were cautious with all their resources and didn't comprehend the idea of cutting up a large piece of material, just to stitch pieces of it back together, and after that be left with bits that could not be utilized.

Ultimately, the Hawaiians discovered a way of using their own clothing fabric (called tapa), which they folded to attain 1/4 or 1/8 patterns, and they provided any waste pieces back to the missionaries for them to utilize in their own quilting. This tapa was from tree bark.

The distinct nature of the Hawaiian quilting is clear in their utilization of local plants, and the spirit world as design influences for their quilts. Conceptually, they utilized quilts to record their surroundings, their departed loved ones, and those still to be born. Their quilts were additionally strongly about the Hawaiian identity and the identity of the individual members of their society.

The Hawaiian Gods, their rites and ceremonies, and their history, are all portrayed in the terrific Hawaiian quilts. Local occasions and significant historic occasions were all perfectly detailed and preserved in their quilts. In fact, all their quilts have a story to tell, or an individual to illustrate, or an act to preserve for posterity.

Quilts were not made in Hawaii simply to keep the women occupied or as a required domestic task. Quilts in Hawaii are their history, and they predict the future as well!

Among the few countries to produce popular quilts that were never ever meant to keep them warm during the night, the Hawaiian culture and history have actually instead been maintained wonderfully. Quilts continue to be made in Hawaii, with brand-new styles continuously emerging. Here, quilts are both the history and the future in a really distinct and important way.

The United Kingdom

Clearly, a chillier environment than Hawaii, the traditions of 'make do and fix' were such that for centuries, the cloth was extremely important and not to be squandered. Long before any mechanical cloth production, each piece of cloth was made by hand or with straightforward weaving frames. Anything so lengthy to produce might just be treated with care and considered to be of worth.

Long before the initial settlers appeared in America, British women and men were engaged in patchwork and quilting, both for home and industrial benefit. So the history of quilting in Britain goes way back.

There are records of padded clothes being produced for soldiers to be worn below their armor to safeguard them from the metal, and additionally to supply heat and comfort. And as far back as the fourteenth century, quilted fabrics were utilized as bedcovers and clothing.

There are instances of eighteenth-century pieces of clothes that remain from honorable and royal households. For instance, an underskirt for a Scottish wedding is now aspect of the Heritage Collection of the Quilters Guild, and dated at 1764.

Although in the homes run by nobles and royals, there were fantastic examples of elegant and splendid pieces of quilting, these were the minority.

The extremely rich would import cloth from abroad and utilize it to show their wealth and social status.

For this reason, we see silks, satins, velvets, and printed Indian calico utilized in intricate quilting, frequently as backgrounds to embroidered hangings and bed drapes. These pieces would usually be made by professional artisans who would have been members of a few of the early Guilds. Women would not normally have been employed on an industrial basis in this way up until much later on.

In the houses of the less well off, the quilting and patchwork traditions would have a lot more practical approach, and although some would be really skillfully designed and executed, the primary issue was to supply heat without excessive expenditure.

The cottage market was very much part of northern England and Welsh tradition, and as such, there would be quilters carrying out work on a commission basis, and either offering directly to particular wealthier homes, or through a representative.

In Wales and some parts of England, there were additionally traveling workers. They would take board and lodging in a home and would be required to supply brand-new quilts for bedding, in addition to other stitch work in exchange for their keep.

In Victorian times, fashion dictated making use of a great deal of rich colors. Fabrics were more readily offered and there was greater wealth available in the brand-new middle classes. Drape and bed coverings that had actually formerly been seen just in the homes of the nobility were now replicated by the brand-new professional and industrial classes.

Many girls of 'great' homes would be raised to be proficient, at the very least, with their needle and thread. So the practice of embroidery, patchwork, quilting, and appliqué was very much perpetuated.

Nevertheless, by the start of the twentieth century and the outbreak of war, things were starting to shift.

When war broke out, women discovered they needed to work to help the war effort. This indicated little time for pastimes, and rationing implied that everybody focused on getting ample food to feed the household and getting domestic requirements.

There was little time or energy for needlework as a pastime. By the end of the 1940s, things had actually started to back to ordinary, the nation was ending up being increasingly more dependent on manufactured clothes and bedding.

Factories had actually emerged throughout the UK, and imports started consequently to add to a big amount of manufactured products.

Truly it was the revival of quilting emerging from the United States that helped Britain reanimate its quilting traditions. Now the Quilters Guild has an important function in supporting quilting in the UK. The Guild established a British Quilting Study Group in 1998, and this supplies indispensable assistance to the quilters these days with research and information.

British quilting has, nevertheless, never ever managed to equal the art of the American quilting traditions, and America has actually been completely responsible for getting the word out and the work of quilting throughout the world as far as Australia, Japan, South Africa and Europe.

Were it not for America; the UK might have let its quilting history disappear. Luckily, nevertheless, it has actually helped to revitalize quilting both as a pastime and as an art form.

Australian Quilting

Women were provided the materials and tools to make patchwork quilts on the way to their Australian destination so that they might sell them and have the ability to support themselves when they landed.

Unfortunately, only one of these appears to have actually made it through, but it is clear that the British women brought with them the abilities and customs of quilting.

Quilting was believed to be an 'appropriate' profession for a woman, and the quilters quickly started to put their work together at exhibits, and a market in quilts was rapidly developed. The British customs were kept, and quilting in Australia continues to regard and reflect the styles and patterns of the mother country.

Nevertheless, for several years, Australian households were extremely poor, and usually, the women were responsible for 'making' all the bedding, in addition to all the clothes and home fabrics. In the absence of cash to purchase great cloth, the ladies utilized their initiative. They utilized old sacks, old grain bags and anything that could be utilized to offer heat. With luck, they would have the ability to locate or get something to make a bed cover more appealing, and the sacks would be utilized as the wadding or batting. The old cloth would be cut and sewn either directly onto the batting, or as a face fabric, and whatever creative talent the maker had would be utilized.

Eventually, it ended up being commonplace to acquire old sample books from traveling salespersons. Numerous quilts were made with suit cloth, along with old curtains, and whatever else was accessible.

Regretfully, nowadays, Australian ladies tend to be too busy to do a lot of quilting. And naturally, with the much more inexpensively available products, it's now a time to purchase brand-new and discard the old. Not like the old days, which exemplified the make do and fix slogan.

Japanese Quilting

Japanese quilting is renowned for its strong spiritual and religious influences.

Quilts were strongly valued and provided as markers of regard to the emperors and ruling warriors. The receiver of a quilt is being wished a long life, and the offering of quilting fabric is instilled with spiritual importance.

The Japanese have actually generally worn quilted garments, especially coats and home gowns. The most popular are the Yosegire patchwork quilts from the 16th Century, which are made utilizing fabric strips. These are still made and worn today, and supply both heat and luxury. Now Japanese quilts have terrific appliqué and embroidery, and have actually continued to be considered of excellent significance.

The French Tradition

Just like the United Kingdom, the recent revival of interest in quilting is truly an outcome of the way the American craft market has actually captured the world since the 1960s.

Although in a domestic sphere, there has actually always been quilting and needlework in France, this had mainly been lost as an art form. The holding of a significant exhibit in the 1970s, which grabbed the imagination of lots of Parisians, and the opening of a quilting and patchwork store in the center of Paris was the start of a brand-new life for quilting in France.

Over the last thirty years, quilting has actually thrived in France, and from being an odd pastime, with materials and tools being tough to discover, it has actually ended up being a progressively substantial business.

The design of quilts in France is, as you would believe, of significant importance. Both standard and modern designs are incredibly popular now. Little and really elaborately worked pieces have a specific charm and are extremely regarded.

The appliqué work, especially the Baltimore style, and the patchwork form, are actually the most popular here. The matelasse kind of quilting is actually popular. This utilizes an entire piece of fabric with the quilting lines drawn on, and after that assembled with a plain backing piece and main padding, and held tight on a frame for the stitching. The top fabric may be silk or finely woven and printed cotton. The design markings are followed with an easy running stitch, but really finely stitched. The patterns are straightforward when taken one by one, yet the pieces are extremely densely stitched, so the end product is really abundant and heavily worked.

These make terrific bed coverings, and the style is utilized for less expensive manufactured pieces which have actually now acquired a substantial market throughout Europe.

There is a significant yearly festival, which is successful in luring over 17,000 individuals from all over the world. Over 800 quilts were shown at the most recent program, so you can see how seriously the French are now taking quilting!

The Piquré de Marseilles is additionally extremely popular, and was made from 2 pieces of fabric, and a backcloth and a fine silk or cotton front piece. The pattern was worked with backstitch, and the filling was placed in between the needle holes.

The patterns are not different from those of William Morris, popular for his Arts and Craft Movement in the UK. The technique was modified later for ease of working, and running stitch utilized instead of backstitch, and more padding utilized to fill out the spots in between the patterns. The stitching work is usually carried out in a contrasting color to the face fabric, and this kind of quilting makes fantastic cushions and products of clothing, like evening jackets.

The boutis progressed to show progressively bigger areas of pattern, which might be done much quicker. The name of this kind of quilting originates from the Provencal for stuffing. The Provencal style was additionally part of this tradition, and local flora and fauna, along with religious and romantic styles, were utilized, reflecting the interests and sensations of the young women quilters.

Later on, primarily white cotton was utilized, and these stunning pieces are popular for being as terrific on the back of the fabric as on the face. The plain white bed covers, pillow covers and throws are searched for, and comparable styles discovered in numerous stores like Laura Ashley in the United Kingdom. The style was additionally utilized for baby clothes and cot covers. The style, although without the padding, has additionally ended up being a classic for great quality underwear.

Regretfully, this style of work is less frequent nowadays, yet fashion trends can regularly surprise, and it might be that it is making a comeback. Although it's referred to as a French Provencal style, it does obviously come from Sicily at some time throughout the Middle Ages.

South African Quilts

With a warm environment, you would not think of quilts being required to keep warm. Nevertheless, they are utilized to illustrate the history and the culture of South Africa.

There is, for instance, a quilt made by Phina Nkosi, who works with the Zamani Quilting Sisters in Soweto. This group formed to try and assist women who not just needed to reside in a racist society, but additionally an extremely sexist one. This group worked on the principle of self-help, and opened a women's resource center.

This quilt consists of portraits of women she thought were part of the battle for liberty in South Africa. The quilt is hung in the MSU Museum Accession, and was purchased in conjunction with the South African Cultural Heritage Project.

The United States of America and Canada

Possibly the most widely known quilting is from this region of the world. In the northern states and Canada, quilting has actually been part of a really strong tradition in domestic arts and crafts, guaranteeing American and Canadian households had both gorgeous and functional fabrics in their houses.

Nevertheless, it is most certainly the stuff of myth and legend that quilting was prevalent, either for practical or ornamental factors, in the early colonial times.

The initial settlers worked hard and long, and there was little time spare for the creative quilting that we erroneously connect to these early days. Nowadays, plain cloth and wadding would have been utilized to reflect the limiting religious beliefs of a lot of the settlers for whom the decoration was considered improper.

These early colonial women would need to weave their own cloth, and carry out all the other domestic duties-- and apart from the reality that the men were considered above such modest work, they had a tendency to be outdoors in the fields, tending the huge livestock, and building or fencing.

Women's lives were hard, and, at first, frequently lonesome. They had poor access to civilization, typically settling in separated locations, with near neighbors probably miles away.

Just later on, as households and farms ended up being more established, and the community facilities developed, were women in a position to have the time and leisure to quilt. Even then, it was mostly in the better-off houses where domestic assistance was brought in, that the lady of the house would do the ornamental quilting.

Naturally, women settlers would bring with them the abilities gained from their families, so a range of styles and patterns were imported by them to America.

However, there was only a really limited amount of fabric available in the early days, and it wasn't actually up until the mid-1800s that there was fabric available for quilting to be economical. Before this date, many families utilized blankets-- of differing quality and heat, but nonetheless more affordable than quilts.

The colonial-style underwent a revival in the twentieth century. The designs of homes, of furnishings, and the soft furnishings all ended up being incredibly popular, both in America and abroad. The concept of 'old colonial-style quilts' was part of the marketing performed by publications and makers, yet the quilts they were marketing were certainly made much later than they recommended, most likely from the 1850s.

About this time, the manufacturing industry was ending up being established, and women in America discovered that they might purchase materials. Those who had sheep for wool and grew cotton, might get the raw materials formed into a fabric, and no longer had the difficult, and lengthy job of weaving and fabric making.

This provided women more time for other things, amongst them obviously, was quilting. So this is actually the moment where American quilt-making actually became a reality.

Patterns appeared and could be purchased in publications or in stores, however, American women took pleasure in utilizing the patterns that their family and friends utilized, and pattern sharing was the standard, instead of purchasing brand-new ones. These patterns ended up being the conventional American quilting patterns that are still popular today.

Quilting was not a simple pastime for lots of women. Space in the homes of the majority was restricted. The quilting frames were typically big enough for at least 6 women to operate at, and at first, were homemade.

Many homes didn't have extra space for the frame, so it would both be assembled, and after that, taken apart as required, or linked to a pulley system and hoisted up to the ceiling when not being utilized.

The quilting bees that made it possible for women to get together were restricted to the variety of individuals who might fit in the available area around the frame.

Chapter 2: The Technical Bits

There are various designs of quilting, which mainly reflect the native land and traditions of their quilting history. Effectively, quilting needs a sandwich of fabrics. You start with a face fabric, which can be comprised of patchwork or blocks, or which might be a plain color, or a printed fabric.

The padding, or batting, used to be placed in between the sewn spots in some old quilted pieces, like quilt surrounds for wall hangings that were mainly works of top quality embroidery.

Nevertheless, nowadays, and especially for bed cover quilts, there are 3 layers. The top layer, which, if it is patchwork, will have been comprised individually of little pieces of fabric joined together to make blocks or parts. The blocks or parts are then sewn together. When the size or overall style has actually been attained, this is then assembled with the batting and back fabric, and the quilt is developed by sewing the 3 layers together. This ought to truly be described as a patchwork quilt.

Nevertheless, there are a great deal of other sorts of quilts.

If the face fabric tells a story, it is not likely that the base fabric is going to be embellished. The stitching is most likely going to be on the outlines of the figures, emblems or picture aspects of the fabric.

Or, the plain fabric could be wonderfully embellished utilizing just sewing to create patterns, figures, flowers or whatever you like.

If, nevertheless, you are producing a bed cover, or drape, you might wish to utilize the sewing to create the pattern on both face and base fabrics. Machine quilting is now incredibly popular, as it plainly allows quilters to produce work faster than by hand. Nevertheless, depending upon the kind of quilt you are making, it can be challenging to manage, or it may not offer the result that you desire.

Hand quilting is still an incredibly popular technique for many, as it does offer a softer, and possibly more elegant appearance. Once again, depending upon the size, you might require a hoop which will secure a part of the quilt, or if it's a bed cover, you might actually require a frame to stretch out a bigger area of the quilt. The old ones were hand made to fit the space available and the number of individuals who might work on the piece at any one time. You can still create your own. Utilize timber lengths covered in the material so that you can pin your quilt to the fabric and hold it in place.

The ends could be utilized to roll the fabric forwards and backwards so that just the working area is extended.

If you are doing hand quilting, you are going to require quilting needles and quilting thread. Typically, you stitch with one hand, and utilize the other hand beneath to direct the needle back through to the face. The secret is to keep the stitches the exact same length and absolutely in line. They do not need to be minute, yet they do need to all be identical to provide an excellent finish.

You can utilize various colored threads to match the color of the fabric, or contrasting colors, or perhaps colorless thread.

If you are utilizing a sewing machine, a walking foot will guarantee that all 3 layers of the quilt move together-- it is necessary not to enable one part of the sandwich to be more out of sync with the others.

A few of the terms for quilting that you are going to find helpful are provided beneath:

Accent quilting can add a pattern that works with, yet follows, various lines to those of any patchwork.

Achromatic color schemes - utilizing black, white and grey only.

Album quilts-- these utilize a combination of blocks relevant to the maker, the recipient or an occasion, and are generally gifts for particular occasions or situations.

Amish Quilts-- these are extremely simplistic and organized and always functional.

Analogous color schemes-- neighboring colors on a color wheel.

Anchor fabric-- this is utilized when piecing to hold the fabric pieces together when machine piecing.

Appliqué-- not particular to quilting, yet frequently utilized on quilts-- this is the use of smaller sized pieces of fabric, typically making a figure or character, stitched to the face fabric of the quilt. Sun Bonnett Sue's are instances of these.

Different stitches can be utilized-- visible or invisible.

Backing fabric-- as you would assume, this is the base fabric.

Bargello quilting-- the use of fabric strips to provide the appearance of a wave.

Basting is a method of holding the 3 sandwich layers together on a momentary basis. You can tack, pin or utilize sticky spray.

Batting is the middle or wadding layer of your quilt sandwich.

Bearding is when the batting fibers come away and find their way through to the face or base fabric-- it occurs more with polyester wadding.

Beeswax coating on the thread renders it tougher and stops it from knotting.

Betweens are quilting needles, and they are extremely short. Sizes 9, 10 or 12 are usually utilized-- the 12 being longer than the 9.

Binding is utilized to produce the quilt edges. It is necessary to cut the binding on the bias to avoid pulling out of shape.

Blanket stitch-- initially utilized to edge blankets and stop fraying, it is additionally utilized as an ornamental stitch for securing pieces of appliqué

Block-- a part of patchwork, generally, yet not always, square.

Border-- fabric strips utilized in between blocks and/or on the top bottom and sides.

Cats ears-- a block design additionally referred to as prairie points.

Chain sewing- a continuous thread to stitch pieces together without finishing off and re-starting.

Chain stitch-- is an embroidery stitch that looks like a chain.

Charm quilts have just one shape which is utilized consistently while never utilizing the very same fabric more than one time.

Cheaters Cloth-- fabric which seems like it is made from patchwork, but which is, in fact, printed.

Cool colors-- blues or greens

Crazy quilt-- quilt utilizing irregular fabric pieces stitched to structure fabric, and after that, embellished.

Crosshatch-- parallel lines marked on the quilt to help hand stitching.

Cross-hatching utilizes straight lines on a grid-- diamonds or squares or rectangles could be utilized.

Dimensional appliqué-- this stands in relief from the quilt cover, either stuffed or not.

Echo quilting-- lines of quilting that repeat around the edge of a piece or a design.

Fat Quarter is a yard and a half of fabric cut in half to make it possible for a square piece 18" x 22."

Foundation blocks are blocks that are comprised of a lot of little pieces of fabric. The completed block is after that joined to other completed blocks to produce the patchwork face. Try and keep the fabric, preferably, to have the straight grain on the edge of the block.

Frames can be little circular hoops for hand sewing or big rectangular frames for holding larger quilts.

Friendship quilt-- made to be offered to buddies or family and typically having messages or utilizing swap fabric.

Grain-- the line of fiber running perpendicular to the side selvedge.

Hawaiian appliqué-- An approach for putting extremely precise design pieces onto quilt fabric.

Hoops-- big frames to hold the quilt for hand or machine stitching.

Lap quilting-- quilting squares as complete pieces, and after that, joining the pieces when they are all created.

Lattice strips-- strips surrounding the blocks.

Loft-- the spare in between the face and the backing fabrics-- high lofts imply warmer, thicker quilts.

Meandering or stippling design-- this is a design of filling in spots of the quilt with stitch, yet none of the stitching ought to touch. So you can not cross over a line you have actually already sewn.

Marking-- marking the quilt by tracing or freehand to mark where to stitch the quilt. Tailor's chalk or wax is frequently utilized-- soap additionally works.

Medallion quilt-- a quilt with a central design from which the remainder of the design follows outwards.

Millennium quilts - or Y2K quilts-- to honor the year 2000.

Miters-- a technique of measuring diagonals and angles.

Monochromatic-- all one color.

Motif stitching provides a pattern which could be done on plain or patchwork quilting. Motifs enable the quilter to integrate names, hearts, animals, flowers and any item or an abstract pattern.

Muslin-- a really thin plain fabric, frequently utilized as a structure fabric for piecing blocks.

No knots-- No knots are to be observed when quilting. The secret is to yank the knot through to the batting layer so that it could be concealed. When you finish, you are going to additionally need to lose your knot in the center batting. Just like a starter knot, wrap the cotton a number of times around the needle, examine your last stitch hole, and pop the needle back in, and pull it through so that the knot stops in the batting, then cut the thread near to the fabric.

Offhand-- normally, the left hand which guides the needle from beneath the quilt

Outline stitching is, as you would expect, meant to offer an outline, and is attained by sewing about 1/4 away from the seam. By doing this, the quilt is enhanced, as you get, essentially, a double line of stitching, and the other benefit is that the stitching is inside the cut edge, and no seal allowance is required.

Paper piecing-- utilizing paper to connect pieces in a block. The paper is generally numbered or lettered and the pieces are matched, sewn to the paper and the adjacent pieces.

Piecing-- sewing pieces of fabric together-- or referred to as patchwork.

Quilting Thread is a single strand of really solid cotton and glazed to help it go through the batting.

Rocking-- this is the popular approach-- if you rock the needle backward and forward, you ought to have the ability to get about 4 or 5 stitches on at one go.

Sampler-- showing a number of various quilting methods.

Sashing-- fabric strips that splits up blocks.

Satin Stich-- side by side stitching.

Selvedge-- the edges of the fabric where the weave was finished.

Seminole quilting-- developing large pieces of fabric with pieces so that the joined fabric can then be sliced and utilized with shapes duplicated.

Sewing in the ditch refers to sewing really near to a seam where the stitches are hardly noticeable.

Sharps-- fine needles for joining pieces and sewing on appliqué.

Stencil-- utilizing a pre-made shape for transferring styles and motifs.

Template-- a shape for cutting pieces-- made from plastic, paper, sandpaper.

Warm colors-- orange, red, yellows and tans.

Piecing together the structure blocks is most convenient utilizing foundation paper. This is going to need to be marked so that you can connect the fabric matching your number sequence. Each piece needs to be stitched both to the paper and together.

Little stitches (min. 14 per inch) and machine needle size 14 is recommended.

Experts advise utilizing tracing paper for machine stitching, yet not for hand stitching. Other alternatives are the paper utilized in medical examination rooms-- it's cheap and works extremely well. Another alternative is the veggie parchment you utilize in the kitchen area, which some individuals find works extremely well. The tracing paper is going to pull away truly quickly after you have actually produced your block, as long as you utilize little stitches.

Muslin is advised for hand piecing.

Present the incorrect side of the fabric to the central piece to the rear of the foundation paper, making sure you have a quarter inch seam allowance all around.

Machine the paper and fabric together.

After that, take a piece of fabric for an adjacent part, and put the right side of the fabric so that it faces the right side of the initial piece. After that, turn over the structure paper to see the marked side, and stitch on the line in between the first and second piece. After that, when you turn it over, the second piece ought to cover its area with the needed seam allowance.

Next off, lay the work down with the numbers on the structure paper facing you.

Fold the paper on the sewing line you have just done, to ensure that the numbers on the paper face one another and the seam allowance of the initial piece and the primary fabric of the second piece are open. Cut the fabric to the minimum of a quarter inch on the edges.

Patterns could be made from nearly anything. The conventional American patterns work on a block or part, and are duplicated throughout the quilt, with each block being comprised of a variety of pieces. The quilts are, after that, edged to surround the blocks.

Typically, paper and sandpaper have actually been utilized. The benefit of sandpaper is the fabric is going to adhere to it well and not slide. Now you can discover plastic template material that has a lot longer life than paper and does not blunt the scissors like sandpaper, nor does it catch on anything.

So how do you create the patterns for quilting?

Initially, obviously, it depends upon why you are making a quilt, which determines what kind of pattern you would like and what kind of fabrics you would utilize.

For patchwork quilting-- most American Colonial Style, for instance, it's really easy to make your patterns, and you can discover a great deal of examples, with sizes, for you to print off from the web.

Cut paper templates for your shapes, and after that, trace them on to sandpaper (fine gauge) or plastic template material. After that, trace the templates onto the fabric and cut out.

Or, if you are creating a quilt from differing shaped pieces, you can make a big paper or card design, and slowly cut out and assemble parts to match your design.

You are going to need to identify the sequence of sewing to develop each square or part if there are overlapping pieces of fabric. Follow the pointers above for utilizing structure paper, which is numbered to reflect the pieces you utilize to comprise the block.

The art of quilting is truly in the care and accuracy, both in the planning stage, and the stitching.

Nowadays you can purchase wadding to sit in between the back and face fabrics, and stitch through to produce the quilt finish. If you secure the 3 areas, i.e., the backcloth, the wadding, and the face fabric at key points, you can then appliqué the ornamental pattern on the face fabric.

Rotary cutting is more accurate than utilizing scissors. The cutters are incredibly sharp and need to be utilized with care-- absolutely something to be kept out of sight and access for children.

When you utilize a rotary cutter, you require an appropriate cutting mat that will not get ridged from the blade and will not harm the blade either. If you utilize a damaged mat, the cutter can move off course, which might imply that your fabric would not have the straight edge you require. The cutters ought to constantly have their blades closed when not in use, and the guard in place whenever you are not utilizing it.

Even skilled quilters and craftspeople have actually managed to cut themselves, so it is vital to guarantee you have the appropriate mat, that the cutter blade is just open when you are really utilizing it, and that blade and mat are kept clear of bits and pieces. Do beware when utilizing the cutter, and do not enable your attention to wander or you run the risk of cutting yourself, and even worse-- getting blood on your wonderful quilting fabric.

Many people working with soft furnishings of all descriptions have an iron and ironing surface in their work area. Pressing fabric to produce your seam lines makes putting together pieces and blocks that much simpler. Having stated that, lots of people do choose to finger press the edges of the tinier pieces, and when all is said and done, it is individual preference and ability level that informs your choice.

Nevertheless, for rotary cutting, when you need to produce the cross fabric line for cutting, it does make it a lot easier if you utilize the iron. Before you cut the cross line, fold the material selvedge edge to selvedge edge and make sure the material lies smooth with the grain of the material in the fold. After that fold it once again so the initial fold and the two selvedge edges are lined up.

Machine-stitching big quilts could be rather challenging. If you do not have a huge work table that is going to hold the total quilt, try assembling some pasting tables, or support some board on chairs. You will discover it a lot easier to work if the quilt is not catching on the edge of your bench and being weighed down.

You can discover a host of information on 'how to' with quilting, in books, on the web and in craft publications. Nevertheless, it's far more enjoyable to discover somebody who has a level of know-how, and volunteer to work with them on one of their own quilts-- you get experience, and, with any luck, a friendship.

Chapter 3: Quilt Decorating

Appliqué is a really ornamental medium that enables your creative abilities full scope. It's a beautiful way to include personal, or any detail truly, and it's possible to do something extremely simple, or extremely intricate and highly worked.

A few of the incredibly popular American styles are referred to as 'sunbonnet Sue.' Generally, they consist of a bonnet, a triangular-shaped dress with curved bottom hem, an arm, and a foot-- and naturally any ancillary figures you like-- umbrella, duck, dog, kitty, and so on. You can utilize any mix of fabrics, and you can embellish the fabrics with sewing for details, like buttons, shoelaces, dress or bonnet trims, and so on

These are fantastic for bed covers and wall hangings in little girls' bedrooms, cot covers, bedspread, and so on. There are a great deal of ways of using appliqué, and they are all appropriate! The only wrong way, is a way you do not feel comfy with.

You can produce your entire figure initially, and after that, either tuck in the edges as you go-- a toothpick or big darning needle both work effectively-- utilize whichever stitch you choose. On some pieces, blanket stitch will look perfect, and on others, you will not wish to see any stitching so you can utilize a hemming catch stitch or running stitch.

Appliqué is a fantastic way to make tinier wall hangings, where you wish to produce a picture. Let's say you wish to have some simple flowers on a reasonably plain background. Select the fabrics you desire, whether they are contrasting or complementary, and draw out your design. Choose whether you desire any embroidery, or whether you wish to develop a mix of fabric as the background. Then develop your appliqué pieces, padded and backed if needed, but not if you prefer so, and after that, secure them to your background quilt.

Obviously, you can utilize appliqué on all kinds of things, and not simply on quilts.

And you can purchase ready-made themes if you want, and utilize these to embellish plain quilts, and even to conceal any damage. There are a great deal of patterns available on the web or in mail-order catalogues.

You can mix and match with appliqué and collage-- so some pieces are undetectably sewn and others could be plainly in relief, with edges, trailing ribbons, whatever works with your style.

The important point is not to be frightened of trying-- you can put together the majority of your appliqué or collage prior to fixing your quilt-- its terrific fun and really easy.

Utilizing painted or batik colored fabric for quilts is excellent fun too.

Another fantastic way of including your individual ideas and styles into quilts is to utilize fabric that you have actually hand-painted or treated in the batik style. You can utilize the color lines as stitching lines, or integrate stitch patterns with color lines as you want.

Trawl the web, go to your local craft museums, take a look at paintings or designs anywhere and everywhere.

You will discover numerous thousands of ideas about what you may like your quilts to appear like-- or ideas that help you develop your own distinct design.

You can utilize paint, ribbon, all kinds of dressmaking or furnishing shop products, themes, embroidery pieces-- embroidery faces, absolutely anything that crosses your mind.

Chapter 4: Distinct and Crucial Quilts Throughout The World

There are some really popular and really crucial quilts that are noteworthy and belong to history-- whether that is ancient or modern.

Of the more recent is the 'Remembrance Quilt,' made after the September 11th attacks in New York. This was created by first and sixth-grade kids from Roy Gomm Primary School. This is a really patriotic quilt, created to show the flag, and indicates the vital assistance from volunteers in the Red Cross that made a recovery from the September 11th possible.

The Red Cross quilts are extremely popular and have actually been utilized as a fundraising method for many years.

The Red Cross had already got a truly well-known quilt in its 'Signature Quilt.' This isn't, nevertheless, simply one quilt-- it is the name given to quilts created for fundraising, as a means of offering therapy and a way of showing the dedication of the many individuals involved in their making.

It's impressive that the simple Red Cross symbol can be recreated in so many different methods and supply such an important means of assistance to the volunteer movement.

The Red Cross Signature Quilts were initially created in 1918 to raise funds for the war effort. It established the tradition of including the values of volunteer work and community, bravery and care of the wounded and ill. This initial quilt was signed by President Woodrow Wilson and his spouse, Theodore Roosevelt, Helen Keller and Sarah Bernhardt, among others.

The Guicciardini Coverlet is reputedly the oldest quilt on the planet and has actually been dated to the 1300s. Half of it is housed in the Victoria and Albert Museum in London, and the other half housed in Florence, this is really important and thoroughly protected.

The oldest quilting museum is claimed to be the San Jose Museum of Quilts and Textiles in California. This museum has ever-changing exhibits, and instances of some of the best quilting from Hawaii and the Amish and Shaker communities in America.

This is a fantastic exhibit of both the really conventional and the really contemporary pattern designs, and is well worth a visit.

In Australia, in the Eskbank House and Museum Collection, there is a quilt going back to 1893 called The Sutton Family Crazy Patchwork Quilt, yet the actual creator is unknown. This is among the earliest instances of Australian patchwork quilting. There is a quilt created by Mary Mayne illustrating actual locations in a village called Eaton Bray in the United Kingdom-- it's a terrific way of preserving information for future generations.

Mary Mayne additionally created the Winston Churchill quilt that is shown at Bletchley Park when the Enigma Code was broken throughout the war. These are examples of the ways quilts can reflect the lives of actual individuals, real occasions, and real locations.

Chapter 5: Quilts, Births, Marriages and Deaths

Quilts have actually been utilized from birth to death-- to commemorate, to mark life changes, for the holding of memories, and to grieve.

Quilts for infants' cribs are nearly a requirement. If you do not make one for your own infant, an aunt, grandma, cousin or a buddy is most likely to create one for you.

The benefit of crib quilts is their size-- simpler to work with, not so time-consuming-- and a justification to truly go to town with design and capability for a newborn.

Quilts in America were typically made to symbolize an engagement to be wed.

Developing quilts for the newlyweds' home was constantly a cheerful endeavor and an opportunity for the girls to get together, for suggestions to be offered, and the fortunate girl to let the world understand how delighted she was.

Wedding presents-- what better than a quilt. They are markers of your kids' lives and their course into the future with households of their own.

There are numerous really lucky kids who have actually quilts produced for them by their grandmas. Integrating references to the youth life and family, pets, buddies, and locations they have actually lived and gone to. These are irreplaceable and beyond value, and I wish I had had one created for me!

Regretfully too, in death-- in the American civil war, soldiers were typically buried in their quilts, which they had taken with them to keep them warm during the night. Numerous quilts were, obviously, ruined throughout the war, and many were taken as keepsakes by others.

Quilts were created after death too, as commemoratives of the deceased, and to show the sorrow and sadness of the mourners.

Maybe more than any other piece of family linen, the quilt has a function from birth to death and could be as personal or impersonal, as joyful or unfortunate, big or little, vibrant, patterned or plain.

They can be embellished in any variety of ways, and utilizing nearly any sort of fabric, the quilt is both an exceptionally useful and potentially strikingly lovely piece. It is a mix of conventional or contemporary designs, personal choice, and it is a sign of our self, our location and our time.

Fashions apply in the realm of quilting similar to other textiles. We have actually seen the renewal, particularly, of the conventional patterns of American patchwork, and these are truly now considered timeless designs, and, hopefully, are going to continue forever.

The delight of quilting, nevertheless, remains in its variety, and its capacity for the creative ability

of the maker.

The big and complicated patchwork patterns are fantastic, and just as fantastic are the tinier quilts, which can say anything you desire.

They can be about your family, your home, your town, city or nation. They can be about your delights or your misery; your love or your loss.

In California, for instance, there is The Quilt Project, which is part of the Cervical Cancer Program, and which actually has squares created in memory of women who have lost their lives to cancer, or who have actually suffered through cancer but have been lucky enough to beat it and keep on living.

There are additionally quilts assembled to hold the memories of individuals who have actually passed away from Aids or Ovarian Cancer.

They are all lovely pieces of work, and fantastic masterpieces. They are additionally really personal to individuals who have actually lost loved ones, and honor individuals who passed away or suffered.

The quilts are displayed in health centers, hospitals and doctors' surgeries, and are utilized to raise awareness, to raise financing and to assist in promoting more research.

Conclusion

Quilting has a long history, and, it would seem, a great long future. The customs of the early quilters have actually not been lost, and they have been taken throughout the world. The British women took their abilities and customs to the opposite side of the world, to America and to Australia. American quilters in the twentieth century are accountable for carrying this craft into the twenty-first century-- all over the world.

The Hawaiian folks record their history through their quilts and reveal the world their religious and spiritual past and present.

The French have utilized quilting as a medium for their creative drive, and have actually created a few of the most gorgeous quilts, with elaborate and creative stitching.

Japanese clothing has actually customarily consisted of quilt work, and the fantastic silks of the kimono can be wonderfully elegant when appliquéd and quilted.

South Africa, as well, has a powerful love affair with quilting, and the colors and patterns demonstrate the environment, its colors and its wildlife.

There are quilts throughout the world that have actually stayed in the identical household for generations, and there are quilts shown in museums and exhibits, in town halls, in hotels, in company workplaces and in dining establishments.

There are ancient quilts that can now be bought so that their stories and makers can live on. And naturally, there are all the quilts yet to be created!

Quilting can be straightforward or complicated patchwork; it can be the most splendid stitchery on simple or pricey fabrics. You can quilt a little cushion cover, a bed cover, a purse, a small, medium or big wall hanging. You can utilize painted or dyed fabrics, and you can include motifs, appliqués or integrate ribbons, pearls or diamonds.

There is nearly any design, any size and any use for a quilt.

I hope that you enjoyed reading through this book and that you have found it useful. If you want to share your thoughts on this book, you can do so by leaving a review on the Amazon page. Have a great rest of the day.

Made in the USA
Columbia, SC
23 September 2020